Love, Talk, Read
To Improve Your Child's Speech and Language

Quick Tips for Busy Caregivers

Celeste Roseberry-McKibbin, Ph.D., CCC-SLP

D0954309

Crescendo Publishing
Hamilton, ON Canada

GetPublished@CrescendoPublishing.com
1-877-575-8814

Cover By: Valentina Pinova

ISBN: 978-1-948719-35-3 (P)
ISBN: 978-1-948719-36-0 (E)

Printed in the United States of America

10 9 8 7 6 5 4 3 2 1

Preface: What You'll Learn

This book will help you learn how to love, talk to, and read with your babies and young children using easy, quick strategies that will improve their speech and language skills. It should prepare them to succeed in school and, eventually, in life. These strategies can be used by parents, older siblings, grandparents, nannies, child care providers, and other caregivers involved in the child's life.

When our children initiate communication, it is critical to respond immediately with love, affection, and attention. Loving relationships are the cradle of successful learning. We begin stimulating our children's language from day one by talking with them, singing, and even reading books. Starting as early as in infancy, we establish the foundation for conversation.

This book covers the typical developmental milestones of speech and language. When should your child say his first word? Put two words together? What sounds should your young child be saying and at what age? If you are worried that your child might have a speech and/or language delay, where do you turn? When should you be concerned?

You are about to be taught simple, practical techniques for encouraging your child to use longer sentences with good grammar and a new, more sophisticated vocabulary. You will learn how to read effectively with your child to boost her reading skills for success in school. It is optimal to keep infants and young children away from screens of all kinds—especially phones. We'll later discuss the American Academy of Pediatrics' recommendations and summarize the latest research.

Today, expectations of kindergarten children are very high. You want your child to be well prepared, and this book will give you fun and practical strategies for preparing your child to succeed in elementary school and beyond. You'll understand the benefits of preschool as preparation for entering kindergarten.

You'll learn that speaking more than one language is a great gift in that multilingual adults have many advantages in our current world. You'll find out how to increase your child's multicultural literacy, or the ability to interact and eventually work successfully with people from diverse backgrounds.

You'll glean information on…

1. Developmental milestones of speech and language, what to expect, and when to be concerned

2. Responding to your child immediately with love and attention to create a secure foundation for successful communication throughout life

3. Talking: creating conversations using simple, research-based techniques for expanding your child's sentences and vocabulary that work into daily routines

4. Strategies for reading effectively with your child and expanding her literacy skills

5. The consequences of allowing too much screen time for your child

6. Practical strategies for preparing your child for kindergarten by encouraging basic reading, writing, and social skills

7. The benefits of multilingualism and multicultural literacy

A Gift from the Author

To help you implement the strategies mentioned in this book and get the most value from the content, the author has prepared the following bonus materials we know you will love:

You can get instant access to these complimentary materials here: www.lovetalkread.com

1. A list of a child's first 100 words

2. A comprehensive list of the Super Seventy: 70 specific easy, fast, fun activities to further develop your child's speech and language skills!

3. A direct link to my YouTube channel with specific how-to demonstration videos of some techniques discussed in this book

4. A list of free, fast, easy-to-implement activities designed to build fine motor and sensory skills along with language skills

Dedication

To my precious and wonderful son, Mark McKibbin, my angel and inspiration for this book.You are life's best gift from God.

Table of Contents

Chapter One

Getting Started: Creating a Foundation of Love and Security

In this chapter, you will learn:

- The importance of attachment as a foundation for effective lifetime communication

- How to create a foundation of love through physical affection and responsiveness

My husband and I never thought we could get pregnant, but one day I woke up and there was my precious baby boy. Because Mark was a surprise, I read all I could on caring for babies. I read a book which described a research study that followed babies into their twenties and looked at the variables that contributed to happiness in these young adults. It turns out that physical affection shown by caregivers early in life was the #1 predictor of adult happiness.

Physical affection, devoted attention, and love overcame challenges such as poverty, divorce, substance abuse, and other environmental problems. I realized that my number one priority with my own baby was building a foundation with love: responding immediately to his cries and signals, and showering him with physical affection. This would create a secure foundation of attachment, and I could build language skills from there. And, of course, as a speech-language pathologist, I knew I should talk to and read with him - and sing too!

Mark's first year went very well, but then he began getting middle ear infections at twelve months of age. This delayed his speech and language skills early in life. With work and the strategies I am giving you in this book, his verbal skills caught up to and actually exceeded his age level.

But we noticed that he had problems with things like cutting, coloring, riding a tricycle, and reading simple words before he even started kindergarten. In kindergarten, he was at the bottom of his class academically. It turned out that he had dyslexia and ADHD, and some neurological problems as well. Mark received several years of occupational therapy, vision therapy, tutoring, and other special services to help him catch up to his grade level. We worked on social skills as well.

Today, the little boy who couldn't read, write, tie his shoes, ride a bike, or make friends is a 24-year-old who just graduated from University of Oxford with a Master's of Philosophy degree in global health care equity. He has worked for members of Congress (starting when he was 14) and has been interviewed on national TV.

How did we get from there to here? Statistically, Mark's odds were not good at all. Research shows that some children with learning disabilities such as his grow up to become involved with the criminal justice system and suffer from life-long behavior problems. How did that precious baby with the huge hazel eyes and wide smile grow into the little boy with special education needs who has become a brilliant young adult with tremendous potential to make a positive difference in the world?

In this book, I'll share our journey and lots of practical advice for developing your child's speech and language for lifetime success. For all the worried caregivers out there, whether your child is typically developing or has special needs, I offer scientifically supported strategies that really work. I know. As a Ph.D. university professor, practicing speech-language pathologist, and a mom, I see it all. I'm here to help; I'm your friend along the rewarding journey to help your child have a happy and successful life.

We'll talk about typical speech and language development and discuss free, easy-to-implement, practical strategies for building your child's speech and language skills in the midst of your busy daily routine. You'll get special tips on what to do if your child isn't talking clearly. We'll talk about multiple languages in the home and how to prepare your child for a diverse world. I'll share additional fun, motivating ways to improve your children's social skills and get them ready for kindergarten.

Let's get started on our journey!

Tips and Takeaways:

- Love, devoted attention, and physical affection early in life are the most important predictors of adult happiness. Respond to your child immediately to build a bond of attachment and trust.

- Even if your child ends up having special needs, addressing them early in life can lead to successful adult outcomes.

- Love-Talk-Read really does work; it is simple to incorporate the suggested strategies into a busy everyday life.

- Go to YouTube and type in Celeste Roseberry Love Talk Read. Click on the video entitled Building Young Children's Vocabulary Through Repetition.

  https://www.youtube.com/watch?v=aLs-F7B9wQFE&t=17s

  Turn to the Appendix at the end of the book to take the Caregiver Communication Quiz.

Chapter 2

What to Expect: Typical Developmental Milestones of Speech and Language

In this chapter, you will learn:

- Typical speech and language development milestones for children ages 0-5

- Advice on what to do if your child is not meeting age expectations

After Mark was born, I watched him carefully for the emergence of the usual speech and language developmental milestones. He smiled at six weeks old, cooed at three months, and said his first word by twelve months old. Perfect! But then the middle ear infections set in. By eighteen months old, he should have been saying fifty words and putting two together.

But he only was saying ten words and was visibly frustrated by his inability to communicate with us. The middle ear infections slowed down his speech and language development considerably. We couldn't understand what he was saying, and tantrums began to occur. It was so hard and frustrating when I didn't understand what my child wanted, and I cried myself to sleep many nights.

I knew that Mark should be saying 200-300 words by the time he was twenty-four months old, but he was not on track at all. What should I do? We put pressure-equalizing tubes in his ears to heal the ear infections, which helped immensely. I continued to talk and read a great deal, using the strategies I share in later chapters.

In this chapter, I share the typical developmental milestones of speech and language and what to expect from 0-5 years of age. Keep in mind that girls develop faster than boys and children from more relaxed cultures may develop these milestones a little later. The term "speech" refers to how we say sounds. The term "language" refers to areas such as vocabulary, grammar, and social interaction skills.

If you have questions because your child is not developing as expected, consult your pediatrician. It is also highly recommended to consult a certified speech-language pathologist near you for an evaluation and recommendations about the next steps. (please see *How Does Your Child Hear and Talk* from www.asha.org)

It's absolutely necessary to know what to expect at various ages because you can intervene early if your child is not meeting expectations. So, strap yourself in and here come the lists!

Birth-3 months

Startles in response to loud sounds
Recognizes mother's voice and quiets if crying (Mark did this the day he was born—an hour after he was delivered)
Increases or decreases sucking behavior in response to sound
Social smile around six weeks (in response to another person)
Around 2-3 months, coos (e.g., "koo, goo")

4-6 months

Moves eyes in the direction of sounds
Makes babbling sounds with many different sounds including /m/, /b/, /p/
At six months, babbles and repeats sounds (e.g., "mamamamama")
Laughs and vocalizes displeasure and excitement

7 months-1 year

Listens when spoken to
Recognizes words for common items like *spoon, ball, juice*
Enjoys games like pat-a-cake and peek-a-boo
Babbling strings of syllables (e.g., babamonigu)
Communicates through gestures (e.g., holding up arms to be picked up, waving)
Shares books with adults as a routine part of life
Can focus on large, bright pictures in a book

By twelve months old, the child should look at and smile at people, reach to be picked up, respond to her own name, enjoy being around people, and make sounds to get attention. She should be saying one-two words.

1-2 years

Says ten words by fifteen months
Says fifty words by eighteen months and puts two words together (e.g., "more juice," "Mommy up," "Cocoa bark")
By age two, says /p/, /b/, /m/, /n/, /t/, /d/
Follows simple directions (e.g., "Roll the ball" or "Kiss Daddy")
Points to pictures in a book when named
Likes to turn pages and listen to simple songs, rhymes, and stories

Recognizes certain books by their covers and pretends to read books

By 18 months, the child should interact with familiar adults and children, look at you when you talk, point to pictures or objects to show them to you, wave or say, "bye," and ask questions ("Where's doggy?" "What's that?").

2-3 years

Says 200-300 words by twenty-four months old and speaks mostly in two-three-word phrases (e.g., "Mommy pick up" "Cocoa bark squirrel" "No bath!")
Speech is understood by familiar listeners much of the time
By age 3, says: /m/, /b/, /p/, /n/, /t/, /d/, /k/, /g/, /f/, /y/, /h/, /ng/, /w/
Asks for things by naming them ("Balloon" "Kitty")
Follows two requests (Get the spoon and put it on the table)
Points to pictures in a book when named
Holds a book correctly

By twenty-four months, your child should listen to stories, ask for help, take turns talking, and go to people for comfort and affection.

3-4 years

By three years old, should be saying 1,000 words

Asks simple questions involving "Who, what, why, where?"

Talks about activities at friends' homes and school

Uses a lot of sentences that have 4 or more words

People outside the family understand most of what the child says

By age four, should say /m/, /b/, /p/, /n/, /t/, /d/, /k/, /g/, /f/, /y/, /h/, /ng/, /w/,/l/, /j/, /ch/, /s,/ /v/, /z,/ sh/

Identifies some letters and matches letters to sounds

Participates in rhyming games

Produces some scribbles that look like letters

By thirty-six months, your child should engage in short conversations. He should play make believe or pretend games, show emotion, use feeling words like "I love you," and follow two-to-three part directions ("get the book and bring it to me").

4-5 years

By 4 years old, able to say or use around 1,600 words

Pays attention to short stories and answers simple questions about them
Understands most of what is said at school and at home
Tells stories that stick to the topic
Writes letter-like forms
Understands words that involve time (yesterday, today, tomorrow)
Understands sequencing words (first, next, last)
Names some letters and numbers
Uses grammar like family does
Has friends and shares toys and activities
Talks about what happened during the day
Changes and clarifies a message when it's not understood

By 4 years old, strangers should understand 100% of what the child says, even though she may still mispronounce a few sounds.

By 5 Years Old, a Child:

Says 2200-2500 words
Correctly produces most sounds: /m/, /b/, /p/, /n/, /t/, /d/, /k/, /g/, /f/, /y/, /h/, /ng/, /w/, /l/, /j/, /ch/, /s/, /z/, /v/, /sh/, zh (e.g. in bei**ge**), /r/, /th/ (note: /r/ and voiceless /t/ as in **th**umb may develop a little later)
Communicates easily with other children and adults

Understands that other people have different thoughts and feelings than she does and expresses empathy for others

Talks about her emotions and feelings

Has long conversations and ask a variety of questions

Tells simple stories in a logical order

Talks in different ways to different people (e.g., talks to a baby differently than to a teacher)

How to Help

Don't anticipate your young children's needs. Make them do something to get what they want! For example, if they want more cereal, they must point, make a noise, or say "more cereal please," etc. If they aren't producing words yet, pointing is enough.

As I say in several parts of this book, a good preschool is one of the best gifts you can give your child. Preschool experience will expand her language and social skills. It will also teach her classroom routines such as lining up, washing hands, and sitting in a circle. All this will prepare her to succeed in kindergarten!

As stated, if you are concerned because your child is not meeting her milestones, start with your pediatrician. Most importantly, take her to a speech-language pathologist who can help you know if your child's development is on track (check www.asha.org).

If there are delays, early intervention will make a world of difference. I know—early intervention helped Mark develop his verbal language skills from being delayed to being highly sophisticated. In Chapter 4, I will give more specifics about how to do this.

Tips and Takeaways:

- By one year of age, babies should be pointing regularly and saying several words.

- By eighteen months of age, babies should be saying 50 recognizable words and putting two words together into short phrases (e.g., more juice).

- By two years old, children should be saying 200-300 words and speaking in sentences of up to 3-4 words in length.

- By the time children are four, strangers should understand 100% of what they say even though a few sounds like /r/ and /th/ may be mispronounced.

Chapter 3

Responding to your Child Immediately with Love and Attention

In this chapter, you will learn:

- The importance of responding immediately with love and attention during the first six months of your child's life

- How to develop your child's resilience and secure attachment through showing affection and giving fast responses to your child's initiations

- Responsive parenting and how this helps lead to lifetime security and success

As revealed earlier, Mark was a surprise. I knew that research showed that within the first six months of life, it is best to respond to babies immediately with love and physical affection. I knew that neglecting Mark and letting him cry was not an option—at least for me. More than anything, I wanted him to have a secure foundation. I once heard a speaker say that relationships are the cradle of all learning. Today, Mark is a strong and secure human being who treats me like a queen. We are best friends, and he is a resilient and hardworking young adult with a bright future. But it wasn't always easy...

I was raised in the Philippines as the daughter of Baptist missionaries. In Filipino culture, they respond to infants and young children right away, and children often sleep with their parents. Most Filipinos believe in responding immediately to babies and toddlers; and they do not believe in letting them "cry it out." So as a mom here in the U.S., I was very conflicted.

Should I let Mark cry it out and sleep in his own room, even if he cried for hours? Wasn't I catering to and spoiling him? For me as a mom raising a child in the U.S., these were very hard questions. I finally decided to go with my gut and Filipino upbringing: the result has been fantastic. Here I present research-based scientifically-supported strategies for creating a secure foundation of attachment that will serve your child all his life.

From 0-6 Months, Respond Immediately

First, research shows us that in the first six months of babies' lives, it is important to respond immediately to their needs. We need to respond with love, warmth, and physical affection. Don't let the baby cry unattended!

When we ignore babies and do not meet their needs, this creates attachment problems: mistrust, insecurity, and fear. Babies learn not to communicate, and they literally give up trying. Thus, not only do babies learn that the world is an unsafe place, but they learn that communication does not work to get their needs met. This can create major emotional attachment problems later in life and negatively impact language skills as well.

When the baby cries, makes noises, or gestures that he wants attention, go to him as soon as possible. Don't rush in anxiously; instead, be calm, loving, and attentive. Talk to him in a soothing voice. Name his emotions:

"Mark, are you hungry? (pause) Do you need Mommy to feed you? (pause) Here is some milk!"

"Uh oh, someone is scared of the dog. (pick him up and hold him close) Is Mark scared of Cocoa? (pause) I've got you. You are with Mommy now."

"Oh, you don't like that wet diaper, do you? (pause) Here, Daddy will change you now. Let's get that wet diaper off you and get a nice dry one on! There we go! All nice and dry! That's a lot better."

6-12 Months

After 6 months of age, if the baby cries, it may be acceptable to speak to him and let him hear your voice before you physically go over to him. Try talking to him soothingly, even if you are at a small distance away:

"Mark, honey, Mommy hears you. I love you. I'll be over in a minute. You'll be okay. That's my sweet boy."

"I hear that siren too—that's a big noise! Mommy is here. I love you, and I'll be right over to give you some hugs. That siren was really loud!"

Developing Secure Attachment Through Affection

When your baby is older—after he turns one— affection and attention are still important. Your child will love and benefit from being hugged, held on your lap, and kissed. But be sensitive; at some point, your child may feel smothered or overwhelmed. Watch carefully for these signs!

When Mark was three and could speak in short sentences, I told him that it was okay to let me know if he had had enough. One day, my sweet child said to me after a long hugfest, "Mommy, no more hugs and kisses, please." That was my cue! I laughed, thanked him for telling me the truth and gave him some needed physical space. It is very important to help our children learn to set boundaries and to feel safe and accepted when they do so.

When children experience love and attention, they develop a secure attachment. Attachment creates resilience, and this is a foundation for life. Caregivers who foster warm, nurturing relationships with children promote a resilience that protects them from the worst effects of a harsh early environment. We need to be emotionally and physically present and responsive.

I'll never forget one day when I was especially busy and distracted. Mark came up and said "Mommy, give me you!" I laughed and realized the truth of those words.

Highly Responsive Parenting

Paul Tough, when discussing attachment research, said (pp. 32-33) "When mothers scored high on measures of responsiveness, the impact of those environmental factors [poverty, crime, homelessness] seemed to almost disappear...regular good parenting can make a profound difference for a child's future prospects."

Research shows that children whose mothers were responsive were, at one year old, more independent and brave than babies whose cries had been ignored. In preschool, the children of these responsive mothers were the most self-reliant. Early attachment creates positive psychological effects that can last a lifetime.

Other research found that attachment status at one year of age was highly predictive of many outcomes later in life. Securely attached children were more socially competent, better at forming close friendships, more resilient, and better able to deal with obstacles later in life.

Before we worry about talking, reading, and writing, the most important thing to focus on for now is love for and attachment with our children. This is the foundation for everything else.

Tips and Takeaways:

- Respond immediately with love and physical affection to your baby's signals—crying, coos, gestures. Immediate, loving, affectionate response builds trust; ignoring your baby fosters suspicion and detachment which can negatively impact her for the rest of her life.

- Secure attachment early in life is the foundation for success throughout the rest of life.

- Children who are ignored give up and experience negative effects on language and emotional development; they may experience many problems as adults.

Chapter 4

Talk: Building Conversations

In this chapter, you will learn:

- How to establish joint attention as a foundation for speech and language learning

- The importance of responding immediately to a child's initiations

- Scientifically-supported speech and language building techniques such as using extensions, emphasizing key words during routine activities, and more!

Very early in Mark's life, we started working on turn taking. He'd make a noise, I'd respond, and then wait for him to make a noise or gesture in return. Simple conversations, involving give-and-take, had begun before he even started talking! I talked with Mark constantly. In the car, the park, at meal times…the conversation always flowed. When he became a little older, no matter how tired or busy I was, I worked very hard to have conversations with him and not shoo him away.

Despite the fact that he had reading and writing problems in elementary school, his early verbal skills grew quickly. Language testing revealed that at six years, his overall spoken language skills were at almost the nine-year old level. People marveled at his long sentences and sophisticated vocabulary! When he was eleven, he wrote a 100+ page fiction story.

Today he is a gifted writer and speaker who was featured several times on national TV at the Democratic National Convention in Philadelphia when he was just eighteen. He just graduated from University of Oxford with a Master's degree.

Establishing Joint Attention

Talking is preceded by joint attention, or paying attention to the same thing. A child indicates interest in various ways, and we have to be sensitive to it. A child may cry. She may gaze at an object. She might point, or make noises. The sensitive caregiver understands all these small attempts at communication and responds immediately with warmth as often as possible. This builds the foundation for conversation, letting the child know that her attempts to communicate are to be rewarded with attention and love.

To improve a child's joint attention skills, try to stretch her attention a little more each day. For example, she may attend to a book for just 3-4 seconds. That's okay! Keep working at it and stretch her attention to a book to 5 seconds, then 6, etc. Every small improvement is to be celebrated!

Responding Immediately Verbally to Children's Initiations

In the old days, we used to believe in the "waterfall of words." In this paradigm, the adult talked as much as possible whether or not the child was interested. While the scientific community still believes in talking a great deal to children, we now know that there is something even more effective: responding immediately to what the child is interested in. Research shows these immediate responses encourage early speech and language development.

There are several ways to establish joint attention and a small conversation. The first is to notice what the child is looking at and pointing to, and when she vocalizes (makes a noise) or uses words. Then, respond immediately. Here are some examples:

Baby Maria is in her crib watching her mobile and gazing at a sheep. You can notice this and say, "Look at that sheep! It is white and fluffy!"

Mom is shopping at Safeway with ten-month old Landon in the cart. He sees a colorful box of Frosted Flakes and points to it. Mom notices his pointing and immediately says, "Look, there are Frosted Flakes with Tony the Tiger. That's what some kids eat for breakfast!"

Dad is out with Marissa in the stroller, and they pass a neighborhood cat. Dad notices Marissa looking at the cat with great interest and saying, "ah! ah!" He immediately says, "I see that white kitty! How pretty! The kitty is wearing a blue collar."

Grandpa and Jose are at a local park. Jose laughs and says, "Duck!!" Grandpa notices that Jose is looking at a duck some feet away, and says, "That's right, there's a big duck and he is swimming in the pond!"

Mommy and Mark are looking at the church directory (yes, that's us. When Mark was one year old, he loved having me name church members!) Mark says, "who dat?" I say, "That's Gladys. Her name is Gladys Smith."

To recap, research has shown that noticing what the child is interested in and responding immediately to the child's interest is even more effective in building speech and language than the "waterfall of words."

Create a Special Time to Communicate Each Day

We can talk with our infants and small children during routine activities. But it is also helpful, when possible, to create small periods several times a day for special interactions where we focus exclusively on our child (no phones!!!). These periods can involve reading a book, playing with toys, etc. It would be best if there is no background noise. Be at your child's eye level where he can see your face, especially your mouth, so he observes how you make sounds.

Use Extensions: Add Words

An easy, scientifically supported technique you can use any time is called extensions, where we add words to something the child said. You can do this any time and in any language. The use of extensions adds to a child's vocabulary and definitely helps him use longer sentences. Here are some examples:

Child: More juice.

Adult: You want some more grape juice because you're thirsty? Here you go!

Child: Doggy bark!

Adult: Yes, the black doggy is barking and wagging his tail.

Child: Read Thomas now?

Adult: Yes, we can read your Thomas the Tank Engine book as soon as dinner is finished.

Extensions worked so well for Mark such that his sentences were long and sophisticated. When he was two years old, we would be at the checkout stand at the store and he'd say, "Thanks, and have a nice day!" The clerk would get whiplash and say to me, "Did that baby just say that?" I'd just smile and thank extensions!

Encourage Pointing

You can start encouraging pointing when the baby is around six months old. Though most babies don't point till they are twelve months old, it is good for you to point to things to encourage this important milestone.

Emphasize Key Words during Routine Activities

We want to use the same vocabulary words over and over in certain routines. Use short, complete sentences and emphasize key words a little more. Use gestures and repetition!

> (at the tub) Oh boy! Time for your <u>bath</u>! Here's the <u>bath</u>! (pointing to bathtub) Now Daddy has the <u>soap.</u> (picking up the soap and showing it to the child). The <u>soap</u> will get you all clean!

> (at meal time) Time to sit in your <u>chair</u>! (pointing to chair) Oh, your <u>chair</u> is comfortable. Here's your <u>cup</u> (handing cup to the child). Is that Meghan's <u>cup</u>? Yes! Now we will eat <u>cereal</u> (pouring cereal into the bowl). Look, this yummy <u>cereal</u> is for you.

Other Free, Easy Strategies to Encourage Talking

Teach your child to take turns. Pat-a-cake and peek-a-boo are great games for this.

Sing! Use songs with motions.

Give children chances to put objects in and out of containers, line them up, and move them around while talking about what is going on. You can use boxes, margarine containers, and other simple household items.

When your child is a little older, stretch, build on the moment, and ask follow-up questions that expand the child's thinking and learning. You can say things like, "What did you think about that?" "Why do you think....?" "How does that make you feel?"

For preschoolers, you can help children see how ideas and objects relate to each other. Use words such as *similar, alike, opposite, different*, etc.

You can also introduce categories such as *fruits, vegetables, furniture, transportation*. Teaching categories will be very helpful for kindergarten.

Introduce the alphabet, numbers, colors, and shapes.

Ask more *why* questions that help children think through ideas and problem-solve.

Make books with pictures that children draw or that you cut out of magazines or download from the internet. Encourage the child to create a story that you write down. Create a "book" by stapling the left edges of the pages together. Have the child "read" the story to you by talking about the pictures.

Preschoolers also enjoy guests such as neighbors, grandparents, and other children who come to visit the house. Encourage children to have conversations with these visitors. Teach greetings, leave-takings, and simple questions such as "How are you?"

Encourage children to engage in cooperative activities with others such as playing house or putting together a puzzle—activities that promote joint cooperation. Help children put on a puppet show.

Talk with preschoolers about their feelings. Give them words to describe how they feel. If a child has negative feelings like jealousy or anger, share the times when you have felt that way and what you did to feel better. Always reassure children that feelings are not wrong or bad; it is the actions we take that count. Help children find outlets for negative feelings. For example, let them run in the park, jump on a miniature trampoline, or punch a punching bag.

The Kimochis program, created by a speech-language pathologist, is extremely useful for helping young children deal constructively with their emotions. For example, an underlying principle is that "All feelings are OK; all behaviors are not." Check out their website for more helpful tips! (kimochis.com).

Tips and Takeaways:

- We start conversations with babies through developing joint attention—noticing what our child is paying attention to and then immediately responding by talking about it.

- We should respond immediately to what our children are interested in, emphasizing key words and using extensions to add words to what they have just said.

- Teach preschool children basic concepts that they will need for kindergarten and encourage them to engage in cooperative activities and extended conversations.

  Go to YouTube and type in Celeste Roseberry Love Talk Read. Click on *How to Talk to Your Child During Daily Routines*.

  https://www.youtube.com/watch?v=FU-soPAlb3A0&t=95s

Chapter 5

Talk: Lose the Tantrums! Establishing Boundaries and Respectful Behavior

In this chapter, you will learn:

- The importance of choices and consequences

- How to hold the line to prevent future tantrums

- How to enjoy the results of a tantrum-free home

Mark was precious and delightful, but very strong-willed. When he was small, I let him get away with a lot because I literally didn't know what to do. I had been a very compliant child terrified of displeasing adults. But my wonderful little boy was stubborn and often told me "no," insisting on his own way. I didn't want to slap or spank him, but his behavior was sometimes unacceptable, and I let him run all over me.

Other people noticed and remarked on it! I'll never forget the time when he (at age three) argued with me for so long that I finally said, "We are doing this because I'm the mommy and you're the boy!" He burst into tears and said, "I am not a boy!! I'm a super hero!!" It was time for things to change.

One day, right after Mark turned three, a friend put a fantastic book in my hand. This book, *Setting Limits with Your Strong-Willed Child,* transformed my relationship with my son from one of conflict and tears to one of respect, obedience, and peace. Our relationship became so much better because he felt safe; my boundaries were strong and non-negotiable. I learned how to use language to help my son think, listen, and problem solve—and, most of all, obey me. Here is what I learned about using language when my son tested my limits. (By the way, it works with adults too!).

First, I learned that anger doesn't work: consequences do. We can help our young children understand cause and effect. When Mark was three, I kept cassette tapes in my car. He loved the Shania Twain tape, and I played it a lot. Often when I wasn't looking, Mark would sneak into my car and unwind my tapes. They were definitely ruined! One day he destroyed the Shania Twain tape. I said nothing and threw it away. The next day, he asked me to play it. Very matter-of-factly, without anger, I said, "You broke it. You broke the Shania Twain tape. It's all gone." I could just hear the wheels turning in that little blonde head, and he never played with my tapes again. I didn't replace the tape. I let natural consequences teach Mark cause and effect!

Choices and Consequences

Rob MacKenzie, the author of the book mentioned above, says that if you tell a compliant child to do something, they will generally do it to please you. But if you tell strong-willed children to do something, their very first thought is, "And what will you do if I don't?" That was definitely my son! So, I learned to give him choices with consequences.

Example one:

Me: Sweetie, please pick up your toys and put them away.

Mark: No!!

Me: If you choose to not pick up your toys, you may not watch cartoons after dinner. (I made sure he understood.) But if you pick up your toys right now, you can watch cartoons. I'm going to count to 3. If you have not started picking up your toys by the count of 3, no cartoons. 1…..2….

If Mark started picking up his toys, I praised him and said, "Good choice! I am so happy that you obeyed me. Now you get to watch cartoons."

If Mark defiantly did not start picking up his toys, I said, "I'm sorry you did not pick up your toys like I asked. You made a choice to not watch cartoons after dinner. I hope you will make a better choice tomorrow."

Example Two:

When Mark was around five, we were at Burger King after Sunday school. Mark positioned himself at the bottom of the play structure's slide. He was spitting at kids as they came down the slide. I told him to stop, but he continued. I said, "I am watching, and if you do that one more time, we are going home right away."

Mark loved Burger King, and definitely didn't want to leave. But the next time a child came down the slide, Mark spit at her. I went over (again, not displaying anger) and said, "That's it. I told you no spitting or we would leave. You spit at that girl, and now we are leaving."

Mark began crying loudly and promised not to do it again, begging me to stay. But I picked him up, tucked him under my arm, and carried him to the car. We drove home in silence. The next week when we went back to Burger King, he was much better and never spit again!

When Mark would start crying and occasionally have a tantrum, it was so very hard not to give in. But giving in is the worst thing we can do because children learn that we don't mean business and that they can control us. This sets the foundation for conflict, disrespect, and bad behavior in situations with other people like teachers at school.

Holding the Line Will Pay Off

It is so hard to be strong and hold the line, but it is crucial. I never got openly angry when Mark deliberately disobeyed me, but I held the line in all situations and followed through with the promised consequences. It wasn't long before he realized that I meant what I said and was not going to give in. Sometimes we have to do this for some weeks, but eventually children realize that we are in charge, not them.

Once more, they feel much safer and happier when they realize that we are in control. Too much freedom is not good for children, and it is very unhealthy for them to feel like they control us. As one book said, if we don't tell our children "no," eventually someone will. And hopefully that won't be the police.

Again, our home and our relationship were transformed when I used words, choices, and consequences to teach Mark cause and effect. When things became more harmonious and peaceful, we were able to have so many more happy times together. My little superhero learned that yes, he really was a boy and that Mommy was in charge!

Tips and Takeaways

- Never slap or spank children. Always use words to shape their behavior.

- Set boundaries on your children's behavior by giving clear, understandable choices and consequences. Make sure they understand what you said.

- If your child defies you, don't respond in anger. Follow through with your consequence and do not give in. In time, your child will respect you more and life will be much happier and more peaceful.

Chapter 6

Encouraging Clear Speech

In this chapter, you will learn:

- How to cover the basics like having your child's hearing checked

- What sounds most children are producing at what ages

- Fast, fun, easy tips for helping your child speak more clearly

When Mark was small and had so many untreated middle ear infections, it was super hard to understand what he was saying. A bright child who got very frustrated, he would sometimes throw tantrums when he wasn't understood. I remember crying myself to sleep one night and thinking, "I wish SO much I could understand what he was trying to tell us!" When we got tubes in his ears, his speech became so much easier to understand. Moving him to a large preschool with children of different ages helped too because he had to learn to communicate successfully with a much wider age range of children.

Cover the Basics

If you are having difficulty understanding what your young child is trying to say, you may check with a speech-language pathologist to see if he needs therapy. The general rule is that when your child is two, people should understand about 50% of what she says. When she turns three, strangers should understand around 75% of what she says. By the time your child is four years old, strangers should understand 100% of what your child says, even if he produces a few of the harder sounds (e.g., r, s, th) incorrectly.

Have your child's ears checked. Like Mark, your child may have middle ear fluid that causes him not to hear everything clearly. Children will talk like they hear! If your child is having middle ear infections, antibiotics alone will not clear the fluid out of his ears. Check with your doctor to see if your child needs something called pressure equalizing tubes to drain out the fluid so your child can hear better.

Have Reasonable Expectations—Typical Speech Development Milestones

We may be expecting too much or too little in terms of our children's pronunciation of sounds. With some exceptions, of course, here are the sounds you can expect your child to say by various ages:

By age 2: /p/, /b/, /m/, /n/, /t/, /d/
By age 3: /m/, /b/, /p/, /n/, /t/, /d/, /k/, /g/, /f/, /y/, /h/, /ng/, /w/
By age 4: /m/, /b/, /p/, /n/, /t/, /d/, /k/, /g/, /f/, /y/, /h/, /ng/, /w/, /l/, /j/, /ch/, /s/, /v/, /z,/ /sh/
By age 5, your child should correctly produce most sounds: /m/, /b/, /p/, /n/, /t/, /d/, /k/, /g/, /f/, /y/, /h/, /ng/, /w/, /l/, /j/, /ch/, /s/, /z/, /v/, /sh/, /zh/ (e.g. in bei**ge**), /r/, /th/

Note: sounds that may develop a little later include /r/ and voiceless /t/ as in **th**umb. Consonant clusters (e.g., <u>sp</u>ring, la<u>st</u>) may develop a little later as well.

Fun General Activities to Warm Up the Muscles for Clear Speech

Just as athletes warm up before a race or game, we can help our children warm up their muscles for clear speech! Here are some fun, engaging ways to do this:

*Yawn or fake yawn to streeeetch those muscles. Make funny faces and laugh!

*Make animal noises. My personal favorite is the "monkey noise"—"uuu—eee, uuu—eee."

*Pretend to be a motorcycle or car and make vibrating "bbbbb" noises with the lips.

*Pretend to be a jackhammer and have the child repeat "t-t-t-t-" or "d-d-d-d-".

*If your child has trouble with /f/, /v/, or /s/, blow bubbles in water or juice using a straw".

*Sing!

*Drink a thick milkshake or smoothie through a straw to warm up that tongue!

Quick Tips for Encouraging Clear Speech

- Try to be face to face with your child at her level where she can clearly see your face and lips as you talk. It is unrealistic to do this all day, so create special times where you talk to and read face to face with your child.

- Hold an object or picture by your mouth. Encourage your child to look at your mouth as you enunciate the word. "Look, Mark, Mommy is saying Thomas the Tank Engine!" You can point to your lips to increase your child's awareness of how sounds are produced.

- Position yourself and your child in front of a mirror. Have fun! You can read a book or talk and do something like the item above. "Look! Bear in the Big Blue House. Look at how my lips go together for those "b" sounds!"

- If you suspect that your child has difficulty hearing, say and read things close to their ear. I did this with Mark when he had middle ear infections and it was very helpful! Try to do this in a quiet environment with no background noise.

- It is EXTREMELY important to not force the child to imitate you. If they do, celebrate! Reinforce them and make a big deal of it. "Wow!" (clapping) "Yay! You put your lips together for "b" just like Mommy did!" But again, do not force them to imitate because they may become turned off to these activities.

- Use "echo microphones." Children love hearing themselves! These are easily available online. Get an echo microphone for yourself and have a fun conversation!

- If your children enjoy it, you can gently touch their lips or cheeks to reinforce sounds. For example, for sounds like "b, m, p, w", you can gently put their lips together to make the sounds.

- Teach basic anatomy of speech. Yes, anatomy, LOL. Teach basic concepts such as lips, cheeks, teeth, tongue, and the roof of the mouth. This will suffice for now.

- For sounds at the child's appropriate developmental level, use a lollipop to touch parts of the tongue and mouth to indicate where their tongue goes for certain sounds. For example, your child might say, "t" instead of "k" (Where are the teas to Drandma's tar?) Using the lollipop, touch the middle of your child's tongue and then the roof of their mouth. Say, "When you say "k," you lift the middle of your tongue to the roof of your mouth."

- Use a concept I call MOOSE: Move your lips — Open your mouth wide — Over-enunciate sounds — Slow down — Elongate vowels.

- Play a game of "Silly Speech" where you and your child talk or recite poems using MOOSE. This is very helpful in increasing your child's overall awareness of clear speech.

Tips and Takeaways

- Children develop sounds at certain ages. Be sure to have reasonable expectations!

- Do fun warm-up exercises to get ready to speak clearly!

- Employ simple and fun activities and methods to improve clarity of speech.

- If you're still concerned, check with a trained speech-language pathologist to ensure that your child is on track. If she isn't, seek early intervention.

Chapter 7

Talk: Exposing Your Child to Multiple Languages and Building Multicultural Literacy

In this chapter, you will learn:

- How to expose your children to more than one language to build their multilingual abilities and give them an advantage in the workforce

- How to increase your young child's multicultural literacy for improved interaction in our increasingly diverse world

Mark's earliest best friends were Mexican American (when he was one), White (when he was two), and Chinese American (when he was five). When he was five, we ran across some gentlemen of color playing banjos in a local park. We had never seen them before. I stayed about twenty feet behind as Mark confidently walked up to them and started a conversation. One remarked, "For a little White kid, he sure is comfortable coming up to us and talking with us even though we're strangers!" Mark has traveled to over twenty countries and feels very comfortable moving in international circles. Unfortunately, he didn't learn a second language when he was little because we didn't have the resources. Ah well, the translation app on his phone will have to do!

The Benefits of Being Bilingual/Multilingual

An unfortunate myth is still circulating in some parts of society: it is confusing for a child to be exposed to more than one language at home. Nothing could be further from the truth! Being multilingual has multiple advantages for both children and adults.

Research clearly shows that children from multilingual homes are more cognitively flexible and have better vocabularies, phonological awareness, memory, creativity, mental flexibility, and problem-solving skills than children from monolingual homes. It is ideal for children to be exposed to multiple languages from day one (Roseberry-McKibbin, 2022).

It is definitely OK for a child to hear a caregiver switching back and forth between languages. For example, it does not confuse children to hear a caregiver say, "Me gustaria manejar. I'll take the car. Muchas gracias!"

Practical Tips for Encouraging Multilingualism in the Home

- If you only speak one language, play songs in other languages for your young child to hear.

- If a caregiver (e.g., a grandparent or nanny) speaks only the first language (e.g., Spanish) and not English, take advantage of it! This individual can speak to your child only in their first language. The person can look at wordless books with your child and narrate them in their first language.

If there is a preschool nearby where other languages are encouraged and/or taught, enroll your child there. The earlier in life children are exposed to multiple languages, the better off they are. When your child enters kindergarten, try to take advantage of any bilingual programs if they are conveniently nearby. One of the best gifts you can give your child is that of being a fluent bilingual (or trilingual!).

Today's workplaces actively seek workers who speak multiple languages. If your child grows up to speak more than one language fluently, she will have a huge advantage in the job market.

Increasing Your Child's Multicultural Literacy

Diversity is so important in society today. As much as possible, you can expose your child to people of different:

- Ethnic backgrounds

- Linguistic backgrounds

- Socioeconomic backgrounds

- Ages/generations (e.g., Baby Boomers, Gen Xers, Millennials, Gen Z) (*note: spending time at a place of worship and with extended family members is very helpful here)

- Religious beliefs

It is important to expose your child to those who are differently abled as well. They can benefit from exposure to people who are in wheelchairs, who are deaf/hard of hearing, etc. It is important for your child to see these individuals as viable, contributing members of society.

Take your child to as many community events as you can. If travel is an option, this is ideal for broadening your child's exposure to diverse individuals.

Tips and Takeaways

- Speaking more than one language has multiple advantages that last a lifetime. Expose your child to multiple languages from day one!

- Increase your child's multicultural literacy by exposing him to people who are as diverse as possible in multiple areas: age, religion, and others. This will help prepare him succeed in a diverse workforce when he is an adult.

Chapter 8

Read: Practical Strategies for Building Pre-Literacy Skills

In this chapter, you will learn:

- Foundational suggestions for encouraging reading in young children

- How to CARE: Comment, ask questions, respond, and extend

- The importance of building print and phonological awareness skills

I had literally read to Mark from day one, and as a baby and toddler he loved books, especially Thomas the Tank Engine. He went to high quality preschools, and started kindergarten when he was almost 6. Though he had dyslexia and ADHD, we overcame these issues through therapy and lots of hard work. All that reading in early childhood was paying off, and in 3rd grade, Mark turned a corner and began reading at a 5th grade level. Today, he reads sophisticated books on politics, philosophy, religion, history, and other esoteric topics. He wrote his own 100+ page fiction book at the age of eleven. He is a gifted writer who has worked for members of Congress. Let's hear it for reading Captain Underpants at bed time in kindergarten!!

Foundational Suggestions

It is never too early to start reading: begin the day the baby is born! Books should have bright, colorful pictures and not too much print on one page. Get sturdy books that babies can chew, handle, touch, and even throw.

Children need to see the adults around them enjoying reading. Children do what their role models do. If you are glued to your phone, your child will want the phone! If he sees you enjoying reading books, he will be excited about reading as well.

Digital books are distracting—most experts highly recommend paper. More will be said about this in the next chapter.

Make reading exciting and fun by using silly, dramatic voices. Be expressive! This is especially important for young children with limited attention spans. Read books your child is especially interested in. In kindergarten, Mark started hating reading and would have none of it because dyslexia made reading very hard. He would let me read aloud to him, though, and all he wanted to hear was Captain Underpants stories and Bible stories with bad guys (there are plenty of those!) Oh, and he liked the Dumb Bunny (by Dav Pilkey) books as well. Sound effects and funny voices kept him attentive and engaged.

I kept reading aloud to Mark, even after reading became easier for him. This helped him enjoy books beyond his independent reading level and expand his vocabulary by being exposed to new words.

Make reading a priority. Bedtime stories are especially good because they help children wind down and relax. Make it a special time of snuggling before they go to sleep. Sometimes children will want the same book over and over—that's fine! Mark's favorite bed time stories as a very young child were *Good Night Moon* and *The Big Red Barn.*

Help your child figure out new vocabulary. Encourage your child to look at illustrations and pictures to figure out new words, but do supply the meaning if she starts getting frustrated. As stated, be willing to read the same books over and over but attempt to introduce new ones once in a while.

Take your child to the local library. Our local library had a sign-up sheet where you could register to read with Delilah the Dog. Mark just loved this, and it was very helpful in the early years when he was struggling with dyslexia.

Comment, Ask Questions, Respond, Extend (CARE)

An easy way to remember how to read with your child is to CARE: Comment, Ask questions, Respond, Extend (add words). You can read the actual book and CARE, or you can just look at the pictures and CARE. Either way, it's effective:

Adult: Look at Thomas the Tank Engine going down the track. (Comment)

Adult: Where is he going? (Ask a question)

Child: He's going to see James.

Adult: Yes! He likes to see his friend James who is the orange train! (Respond and Extend)

Adult: Oh boy, I think James is glad to see him. (Comment)

Child: James happy.

Adult: James is happy because Thomas is his friend and they like having fun together. (Respond and Extend)

Here are some more specific ideas for building your child's early reading skills:

Before You Start Reading

Look at the pictures and talk about them. Build pre-literacy skills by asking your child:

1. How do you hold a book?

2. Where is the cover?

3. Who is the author?

4. What do you think the book is going to be about?

5. Point to the first page.

6. Point to the first word.

7. Will you turn the pages with me while we read?

Build on the child's previous knowledge. For example, if the story is about Dogzilla, you can say, "Do you have a dog? Do you know anyone who has a dog?" In another example, "Look at that red fire engine. It has 4 wheels, just like a car. What does your Daddy's car look like?"

During Reading

Ask questions such as:

1. Where should I read next?

2. Where is the page number?

3. Why did the character do that?

4. What do you think is going to happen next?

5. How does this character make you feel?

After Reading

Review the story by asking questions such as:

1. What was the story about?

2. What happened in the story?

3. How did the story end?

4. What was your favorite part of the story?

5. Which picture did you like best? Why?

Build Phonological and Print Awareness Skills

Start building your child's phonological awareness skills—awareness of how words sound. The very best way to do this is through rhyming, and I highly recommend Dr. Seuss books!

It's never too early to build print awareness skills—awareness of how words look. An easy way to do this is to start by having your child track print, or put his finger under each word as it is read. You yourself can put your finger under each word as you read. In Chapter 9, we'll say more about building phonological awareness and print skills.

Tips and Takeaways:

- Read to your child from day one. Use colorful, bright, interesting books with fun textures.

- Be sure to CARE: Comment, Ask Questions, Respond, Extend.

- Remember to be a role model by reading yourself. Children imitate the actions of the adults around them!

Go to YouTube and type in Celeste Roseberry Love Talk Read. Click on the video entitled *Reading Picture Books with Toddlers*.

https://www.youtube.com/watch?v=fAYBmND-lEBo&t=58s

Also check out the video entitled *How to Read to Your Child with Care.*

https://www.youtube.com/watch?v=kjiPM-WM3i00&t=53s

Chapter 9

Zooming with Grandma: Is Screen Time OK?

In this chapter, you will learn:

- What the American Academy of Pediatrics says about screen time

- The importance of joint media engagement

- Impacts of screen time and caregivers' phone use

- The benefits of paper books over electronic books

We very carefully kept Mark away from TV until he was three years old, at which time I began allowing Disney and Bible Man movies. I always watched and discussed the movies with him. Growing up, he was not allowed to play video games. This made it very hard socially with other boys at times, but Mark knew I loved him enough to keep him away from those games. I explained that they were bad for his brain, but we did a lot of other fun activities.

Today, Mark proficiently uses his phone and is a whiz at technology, including website building and social media. He currently works as the social media director for a state senate candidate and a school board candidate. Mark is incredibly creative and funny, and has thanked me many times for keeping him away from video games and phones when he was small.

American Academy of Pediatrics Guidelines

- For children younger than eighteen months, avoid the use of screen media other than video-chatting (zooming with Grandma).

- For children ages two to five years, limit screen use to one hour per day of high-quality programs. Parents should co-view media with children to help them understand what they are seeing and apply it to the world around them.

- Be sure to place consistent limits on the time spent.

- Parents of children eighteen to twenty-four months of age who want to introduce digital media should choose high-quality programming and watch it with their children (joint media engagement) to help them understand what they're seeing.

Joint Media Engagement

- Current wisdom tells us that the less screen time, the better—especially before the age of five. However, if we choose to let our young children have screen time (e.g., TV, phones, iPads), we should always make sure there is joint media engagement. In short, we need to watch the screens with our children and discuss what is happening. Screens should never, ever be used as babysitters!

- The American Academy of Pediatrics has a Family Use Plan. You can go online and type in information about your children (e.g., their ages) and the website will create an individualized plan tailored to your child's individual needs. Go to:

  https://www.healthychildren.org/English/media/Pages/default.aspx

Impacts of Screen Time

Recent research using sophisticated neural imaging techniques shows us that excessive screen exposure can neurologically damage a young person's developing brain in the same way that cocaine addiction can. In one author's words, we are "giving digital morphine to kids." Screens have been called "electronic cocaine," and addiction has skyrocketed in the U.S. and in other countries around the world. Childhood obesity and sleep problems abound.

Stillman and Stillman (2017) tell us that almost one half of Millennials are now parents themselves. There is a small but growing trend for these young parents to limit technology with their children, as the parents recognize the negative effects that technology can have. As Stillman and Stillman said, who knew that crayons and play dough would make a comeback?

It takes great discipline, time, and yes, sacrifice to interact with our children instead of letting technology babysit them. I have been that mom with people glaring at me and giving me dirty looks over my son Mark's behavior in public when he was little. I could just read the "bad mom!" thought bubble hovering over their heads. In those moments, I would have paid $1,000 cash for a phone or other device to quiet my child down in public. I get it. But interacting with our children instead of using a screen to quiet them pays huge dividends in the end.

We were on a plane to Alaska; I'll never forget a young mom with a very hyper one-year old boy who wanted to run the plane aisles for hours. Even I would have brought out a phone in desperation, but this strong, self-disciplined mom was having none of it. She took out some blue masking tape and allowed her boy to tear it into little pieces and stick the pieces on the back of the seat in front of him (yes, she cleaned it up afterwards). She had a vast array of real books and stuffed animals. She talked, read, played, and sang—for several hours. I just wanted to cheer. She is a hero in my book, and though she was very ragged at the end of the trip, her child benefitted from love, attention, and hands-on interaction at great cost to his mother.

Ma and colleagues (2017) studied 1077 children whose average age was eighteen months old. These researchers found a significant correlation between the time the subjects spent with handheld devices (e.g., phones) and expressive language delay. They concluded that small children who have more handheld screen time are at increased risk of expressive language delays.

Caregivers' Phone Use

We know that it is not good to expose infants and young children to smart phones. But are children impacted by their caregivers' phone use?

A recent study linked parental use of smart phones to misbehavior in children. Author Brandon McDaniel has been researching technology's intrusion into face-to-face communication and relationships. He found that the more parents spent time on their phones, the more children acted out in tantrums, restlessness, and hyperactivity. McDaniel emphasized that parents shouldn't feel guilty about needing their phones; however, they need to watch how often they pull out their phones when their young children are around.

Electronic vs. Paper Books

Many caregivers have wondered if it is okay to use electronic books instead of paper or print books with their babies and young children. Recent research about use of electronic books reveals that young children show better focus and comprehension when parents use print books, not eBooks.

Scientific studies have proven that eBooks are distracting to young children. While eBooks initially attract and engage young children more readily, print books still win in terms of children developing better vocabularies, sentence structure, and story comprehension.

eBooks may be useful in elementary school and beyond, but their use with young children is discouraged.

Tips and Takeaways:

- The American Academy of Pediatrics has come up with recent guidelines that discourage use of screens before eighteen months of age except for video chatting.

- Screen time with small children should be very limited; when it is allowed, there needs to be joint media engagement where a caregiver watches with children and discusses what they have seen.

- Current research discourages the use of electronic books with young children, showing that print books increase story comprehension and vocabulary skills and are overall superior to eBooks.

Go to YouTube and type in Celeste Roseberry Love Talk Read. Click on the video entitled *How to Build Literacy Through Talking About Pictures in a Book*.

https://www.youtube.com/watch?v=DtjdxQZu-vy4&t=17s

Chapter 10

School Here I Come: Preparing Your Child for Kindergarten

In this chapter, you will learn:

- The importance of preschool in terms of teaching the "hidden curriculum" of the classroom

- How to increase phonological and print awareness skills

- How to increase simple writing skills

- The importance of reading informational books with your child

- How to promote a growth mindset

Because Mark was an only child, I knew he needed to socialize. From birth to three years old, he was in a small home care environment. When Mark turned three, I realized this was not enough and placed him into a larger preschool which also had an elementary after-school program. Wow, did his language skyrocket! What a difference! And he learned about lining up, waiting his turn, sitting in a circle, listening, and making friends.

I'll never forget going to pick him up one day and seven girls were lined up at the fence, waiting to say goodbye to him. Not bad for an only child with a history of awkward social skills! Right before kindergarten, we put Mark in Montessori. This is honestly one of the best moves I ever made. The teachers worked diligently on his reading, writing, spelling, and phonics. He learned self-discipline and made friends.

Preschool and the Hidden Curriculum

Let's talk about preschool. Should you do it? Anecdotally, here is what I have noticed as a speech-language pathologist. The kindergarten children who have never been to preschool have a rocky road ahead of them indeed, and boy do they stand out!! They have no idea how to line up, sit in a circle, pick up their toys, share with other children, and a thousand other small things we take for granted. We tend to focus on academics: can the child read, write, spell, do simple math?

All of those skills are built upon a foundation of knowing how to behave in the classroom—what some authors have called the "hidden curriculum." When the teacher asks you to do something, you obey immediately; you don't wander off and do your own thing! But a child with no preschool background does not know that, and often is not even ready to learn. Preschool teaches those "hidden curriculum" skills.

Mark, having ADHD, interrupted a lot as a preschooler. He came home and told me that Miss Tonya at Montessori would say to him, "Mark, we're not talking about that right now." She would shut down his extraneous comments and keep talking about the topic at hand. Mark needed that! His kindergarten teacher sure wasn't going to tolerate interruptions and deviations from the topic!

Placing your child in a high-quality preschool is the best gift you can give him to prepare him for kindergarten. What else can you do to get him ready, especially in terms of literacy skills?

Increasing Phonological Awareness Skills

Phonological awareness, mentioned in chapter 8, is the awareness of the sound system of a language. We said that rhyming is the foundation for this. Here are other skills, listed in a hierarchy, that you want to help your child develop before she goes to school:

1. Count the number of words in a sentence

2. Count the number of syllables in a word (clapping is very helpful)

3. Count the number of sounds in a word

4. Identify the first sound in a word

5. Identify the last sound in a word

A wonderful website that helps with these skills is www.starfall.com. I used it with my own son in kindergarten, and it was extremely helpful!

Increasing Print Awareness Skills

We discussed print awareness skills in Chapter 8; this is the awareness of how words look. Before our children start kindergarten, they need to be able to:

1. Display interest in reading and sharing books

2. Identify the front and back of the book

3. Identify the top and bottom of the page

4. Look at the book while turning the pages from left to right

5. Identify the title on the front cover

6. Identify titles of favorite books

7. Distinguish between pictures and print on a page

8. Know where the story begins in the book

9. Identify letters that occur in their own names

10. Print the first letter of their name

11. Recite the alphabet

12. Point to the first and last letter in a word

13. Differentiate uppercase from lowercase letters

14. Use terms such as *letter, word, alphabet*

15. Respond to common environmental signs (e.g., stop, restroom signs)

Simple Writing Skills

We can also work on simple writing skills with children. Writing depends on fine motor movements of the hand, wrist, and fingers. Mark had a great deal of trouble with writing when he was little, and these ideas helped:

1. Make sure your child has plenty of opportunities to scribble, color, and paint. Make free use of crayons, paint, and sidewalk chalk.

2. Activities involving clay and play dough help develop fine motor skills.

3. Have your child trace letters with her finger in clay, playdough, or salt.

4. When your child is reading or watching TV (not too much!!) she can squeeze a squishy ball to strengthen the muscles of her hands and fingers.

5. Encourage writing notes and letters to friends and family members. Remember: perfection is not necessary, but the attempt to write is very important.

Remember to check my website, lovetalkread. com, for more ideas about increasing your child's fine motor skills for more successful writing.

Reading Informational Books with Your Child

Continue to read with your child, providing many different books about different topics. As she gets a little older, you can add informational books to her repertoire. When children are small, we love to read them stories. Stories are terrific, but kindergartens these days place a great deal of emphasis on reading for information.

Mark loved Bob the Builder books as a preschooler. We read about dump trucks, cement mixers, and other topics. I love Byron Barton books, simple and colorful informational books about planes, trains, and other fascinating topics. We can read these informational books with children and ask questions about what they have learned. This will greatly help in preparing them for kindergarten.

Promote a Growth Mindset

Lastly, as your child's language becomes more sophisticated, you can prepare him for school by encouraging what Stanford researcher Dr. Carol Dweck calls a growth mindset. She encourages caregivers to not say things like "You're so smart!" (person praise). Instead, she recommends process praise—praising children for effort and hard work. Dr. Dweck explains that when we praise children for innate qualities (e.g., "you're so smart!") we set them up for failure if they don't succeed. They feel like they failed because they were not really smart, and this makes them insecure.

I discovered Dr. Dweck's research when Mark was around nine years old, and it dramatically changed the way I praised him. Here are things you can say to encourage your child to be more perseverant and resilient, relying on effort and hard work rather than innate talent:

You worked very hard on that. I'm proud of you. That took a lot of effort! Way to go!
You got a good grade because you spent a lot of time working on that picture.
I love how hard you are trying. Trying hard is the most important thing.

Process praise about effort works wonders. I know—I tried it and had incredible success with my own child. I stopped telling Mark he was smart. I praised him for hard work, effort, and perseverance. I am confident that this is a major reason he is so successful as a young adult.

Tips and Takeaways:

- High-quality preschool is one of the very best gifts you can give your child. Be sure to choose a place which emphasizes creative play as well as reading and writing!

- Begin addressing phonological and print awareness skills, developing fine motor skills for writing as well.

- Don't tell your child "You're so smart!" Praise effort, hard work, and perseverance to build a more resilient child who is not afraid of failure.

Go to YouTube and type in Celeste Roseberry Love Talk Read. Click on the video entitled *Responding with CARE: Comment, Ask Questions, Respond, Extend.*

https://www.youtube.com/watch?v=NoRDDsjuZy8&t=22s

Click also on the video entitled Fostering Print Awareness in Preschool Children.

https://www.youtube.com/watch?v=QU1tDWHgy0Y

Chapter 11

Putting it all Together

All of us want our children to succeed and enjoy a bright future. Across the globe, this is every parent's universal desire. We want our children to have a strong start, for we know that an excellent foundation leads to a life of success and happiness.

Although my husband and I did all the right things and plenty more, our beautiful baby had some special needs. Dyslexia, ADHD, and neurological problems were not what we expected from the child of two parents with doctorates. But time, lots of therapy, and patience helped our son succeed and become the wonderful adult he is today. We implemented virtually every strategy you read about in this book. I've shared the how-to's of our journey, and I know that they can work for you as well.

It has been so gratifying to see Mark go from a shy little boy who couldn't read and write or tie his shoes to a confident, brilliant, successful adult who has worked for members of Congress and just finished a Master's of Philosophy at the University of Oxford.

When I see him deep in the middle of a thick book on American history or read his Philosophy class college essays, I am transported back to that night when my six-year old tearfully told me as he cried himself to sleep, "I'm stupid—I'm a loser—I kill myself." How did we get from there to here?

Starting on day one, I responded to Mark with love. I did not let him "cry it out," but rather attended to his needs immediately with love and affection. I gave him lots of hugs and kisses, and held him a lot. I talked to him a great deal, noticing what he was interested in and responding to that in the moment.

I so clearly remember using extensions constantly—both during daily routines and special times like reading a book before bed. When he said something, I'd add words. When he said, "Good Night Moon, Mommy?" I'd say, "Yes, we will read your book Good Night Moon before you go to sleep." Mark's early verbal skills were very highly developed, and I know that my use of extensions was key.

We read to Mark every single day. Even when he began to dislike reading for a few years because dyslexia made it so hard for him, we continued reading aloud. I learned how to use funny voices and be entertaining and engaging!

I learned how to set boundaries with Mark by giving him choices and consequences. When he defied me, I did not become angry and slap or spank him. He was not allowed to negotiate. I followed through with consequences and life became much happier and more peaceful.

When Mark was a toddler with multiple middle ear infections, his speech was very hard to understand. We got pressure equalizing tubes put in to drain fluid out of his middle ears. I read and spoke to him very close to his ear in a slightly louder voice so he could hear me better. I had him watch my face and lips while I talked and read. His speech became so clear that strangers would remark on it.

We put Mark in stimulating preschools with lots of outdoor activities and literacy activities as well. We saw his verbal and social skills skyrocket as he, our only child, spent time learning to relate to children from a variety of cultural backgrounds and age levels. Through church and community events, we exposed him to a wide variety of people across the age span.

Carol Dweck's growth mindset research dramatically altered the way I praised Mark. Gone were statements such as "You're so smart" and "Wow, you're a great artist!" These were replaced by process praise, which emphasized his effort and perseverance. I have often thought that given Mark's special challenges such as dyslexia, we would be at a very different place today without process praise.

He struggled for years with things that came easily to other children. I so clearly remember him crying on more than one occasion and saying, "Mommy, why are things so easy for the other kids and so hard for me?" I would take him in my arms and tell him how special he was and that he was learning to work harder than everyone else. I told him that God wanted him to do special things someday, and that his problems were helping him to learn to work extra hard. Mark knew the word "perseverance" very early in life.

Today, he is a resilient, happy, and incredibly industrious young adult with a bright future. As stated, he graduated from the University of Oxford with a Master's of Philosophy degree and wants to work in the health care industry, helping provide health care benefits to members of marginalized communities around the world.

And I wish you the very best for yourself and your own child. If you are struggling, know that you are not alone and that there is hope. Don't be afraid to seek special help and support if your child needs it. Mark had occupational therapy for two years, vision therapy for 1.5 years, and tutoring at various points from preschool through high school. He has seen a professional therapist to help cope with issues that arise from having ADHD.

Love, Talk, Read really does work. Simple strategies such as those I've described in this book are scientifically supported and have worked so well for my own child. Be consistent and persistent, and your efforts will pay off. And remember, as three-year old Mark said, "Give me you." Your love is the best gift of all.

About the Author

Celeste Roseberry-McKibbin received her Ph.D. from Northwestern University. She is a Professor of Communication Sciences and Disorders at California State University, Sacramento. Dr. Roseberry is also currently a public school speech-language pathologist in San Juan Unified School District, where she provides direct services to students from ages 3-18. She has worked in educational and medical settings with a wide variety of clients, ranging from preschoolers through geriatric patients.

Dr. Roseberry's primary research interests are in the areas of assessment and treatment of culturally and linguistically diverse students with communication disorders. A specialty is service delivery to students from low-income backgrounds. Her Love, Talk, Read book drive that collects and donates books to at-risk children experiencing poverty has donated over 350,000 books in the U.S. and 50+ countries around the world.

The author has over 70 publications, including 17 books, and has made over 700 presentations at the local, state, national, and international levels. Dr. Roseberry is a Fellow of the American

Speech and Hearing Association (ASHA), and the winner of ASHA's Certificate of Recognition for Special Contributions in Multicultural Affairs. She received ASHA's Honors of the Association. She earned the national presidential Daily Point of Light Award for her volunteer work in building literacy skills of children experiencing poverty. She lived in the Philippines from age six to seventeen as the daughter of Baptist missionaries.

Other Books by the Author

Roseberry-McKibbin, C. (2022). *Multicultural children with special language needs: Practical strategies for assessment and intervention (*6th ed.). Academic Communication Associates.

Roseberry-McKibbin, C., Hegde, M.N., & Tellis, G. (2023). *An advanced review of speech-language pathology: Preparation for Praxis and comprehensive examination* (6th ed.). Pro-Ed.

Roseberry-McKibbin, C. (2014). *Increasing oral and literate language skills of children in poverty.* Professional development continuing education program for the American Speech-Language Hearing Association. American Speech-Language-Hearing Association.

Roseberry-McKibbin, C. (2013). *Increasing the language and academic skills of children in poverty: Practical strategies for professionals (2nd ed.).* Plural Publishing.

Roseberry-McKibbin, C. (2007). *Language disorders in children: A multicultural and case perspective.* Allyn & Bacon.

Karanth, P., Roseberry-McKibbin, C., & James, P. (2017). *Intervention manual for prerequisite learning skills: Practical strategies.* Plural Publishing.

Karanth, P., Roseberry-McKibbin, C., & James, P. (2017). *Intervention for preschoolers with cognitive, social, and emotional delays: Practical strategies.* Plural Publishing.

Karanth, P., Roseberry-McKibbin, C., & James, P. (2017). *Intervention for toddlers with cognitive, social, and emotional delays: Practical strategies.* Plural Publishing.

Karanth, P., Roseberry-McKibbin, C., & James, P. (2017). *Intervention for preschoolers using augmentative and alternative communication: Practical strategies.* Plural Publishing.

Karanth, P., Roseberry-McKibbin, C., & James, P. (2017). *Intervention for toddlers using augmentative and alternative communication: Practical strategies.* Plural Publishing.

Karanth, P., Roseberry-McKibbin, C., & James, P. (2017). *Intervention for preschoolers with gross and fine motor delays: Practical strategies.* Plural Publishing.

Karanth, P., Roseberry-McKibbin, C., & James, P. (2017). *Intervention for toddlers with gross and fine motor delays: Practical strategies.* Plural Publishing.

Karanth, P., Roseberry-McKibbin, C., & James, P. (2017). *Intervention for preschoolers with communication delays: Practical strategies.* Plural Publishing.

Karanth, P., Roseberry-McKibbin, C., & James, P. (2017). *Intervention for toddlers with communication delays: Practical strategies.* Plural Publishing.

Shipley, K., & Roseberry-McKibbin, C. (2006). *Interviewing and counseling in communicative disorders: Principles and procedures* (3rd ed.). Pro-Ed.

Connect with the Author

Websites:
www.lovetalkread.com
https://webpages.csus.edu/celeste/

Email: celeste@csus.edu

Address:
Dept. of Communication Sciences and Disorders
6000 J Street
Sacramento State University
Sacramento, CA 95817
Phone: (916) 278-6601

Social Media:
Tik Tok: @celesteroseberry
Instagram: @dr.celesteroseberry
YouTube channel is Celeste Roseberry (Love Talk Read)
Facebook: Love Talk Read
LinkedIn: Celeste Roseberry

Acknowledgements

I would like to thank Robbin Simons and Shayna Rohrig of Crescendo Publishing for this wonderful opportunity to share my vision with a wider audience. Thanks and lots of love go to Dr. Elaine Fogel Schneider for introducing me to Crescendo and facilitating the relationship. Most of all, I thank God, my heavenly Father, for the gifts of life, health, and the chance to communicate my vision to the world.

Resources

Specific Strategies for Improving Your Child's Speech and Language:

www.lovetalkread.com

https://walkietalkiespeechtherapy.com/

https://peachiespeechie.com/

https://www.sunnydays.com/

www.asha.org

http://www.earlyliteracylearning.org

starfall.com

Other Helpful Resources:

https://www.kimochis.com/ (to improve your child's behavior and social skills)

www.cdc.gov/ncbddd/actearly/milestones (developmental milestones in different languages)

http://www.askdrelaine.com (7 Strategies for Raising Calm, Inspired, and Successful Children) https://www.healthychildren.org/English/media/Pages/default.aspx

(to create your own Family Media Plan)

http://www.upi.com/Health_News/2017/06/15/Study-links-parental-focus-on-smartphones-misbehaving-children

Good Toys for Young Children
http://www.naeyc.org

Tips for Attachment Parenting
http://www.attachmentparenting.org/principles/principles.php

Suggestions for growth and development for preschoolers
http://kidshealth.org

Popular resource for educational toys
http://www.melissaanddoug.com

Great source of ideas for developing school readiness
http://main.zerotothree.org
Instagram: thedabblingspeechie

References

Chalko, K. (2021). *How to teach a toddler to talk: Online course workbook*. Available on Amazon.

Duckworth, A. (2016). *Grit: The power of passion and perseverance*. Scribner.

Dweck, C.S. (2016). *Mindset: The new psychology of success* (2nd ed.). Random House.

Fowler, W. (1995). *Talking from infancy: How to nurture and cultivate early language development*. Center for Early Learning and Child Care.

Gold, J. (2015). *Screen-smart parenting: How to find balance and benefit in your child's use of social media, apps, and digital devices*. Guilford Press.

Kardaras, N. (2016). *Glow kids: How screen addiction is hijacking our kids—and how to break the trance.* St. Martin's Press.

McDaniel, B. (2019). *Passive sensing of mobile media use in children and families: A brief commentary on the promises and* pitfalls. *Pediatric Research.* doi: 10.1038/s41390-019-0483-8

Ma, J., van den Heuvel, M., Maguire, J., Parkin, P., & Birken, C. (2017, May). *Is handheld screen time use associated with language delay in children*? Paper presented at the annual Pediatric Academic Societies Meeting, San Francisco, CA.

MacKenzie, R.J. (2001). *Setting limits with your strong-willed child: Eliminating conflict by establishing CLEAR, firm, and respectful boundaries.* Three Rivers Press.

Marklund, U., Marklund, E., Lacerda, F., & Schwarz, I. (2015). Pause and utterance duration in child-directed speech in relation to child vocabulary size. *Journal of Child Language, 42*, 1158-1171.

Ross-Swain, D., & Fogel Schneider, E. (2018). *Confidence & joy: Success strategies for kids with learning differences: A step-by-step guidebook for parents and professionals.* Crescendo Publishing.

Schneider, E.F. (2016). *7 strategies for raising calm, inspired, and successful children.* Crescendo Publishing.

Stillman, D., & Stillman, J. (2017). *Gen Z @ work: How the next generation is transforming the workplace.* HarperCollins Publishers.

Tough, P. (2016) *Helping children succeed: What works and why.* paultough.com.

APPENDIX
Caregiver Communication Quiz

Name of Caregiver_____

Relationship to Child_____ **Date**_____

1 = never 2 = not very often   3=sometimes
4 = often   5 = always

For each item, circle the one that best reflects your current practice. It's OK to have room for improvement!

1. When my child cries or tries to communicate in some other way (e.g., pointing), I respond immediately.

    1 = never 2 = not very often   3=sometimes
    4 = often   5 = always

2. If my child tries to get my attention and I'm on my phone, I try to get off and attend to my child right away.

    1 = never 2 = not very often   3=sometimes
    4 = often   5 = always

3. When I take my child to places, I talk to him in the car.

   1 = never   2 = not very often   3=sometimes
   4 = often   5 = always

4. I introduce my child to new people and situations on a regular basis.

   1 = never   2 = not very often   3=sometimes
   4 = often   5 = always

5. I read to my child every day.

   1 = never   2 = not very often   3=sometimes
   4 = often   5 = always

6. I spend special, One-on-one time with my child every day.

   1 = never   2 = not very often   3=sometimes
   4 = often   5 = always

7. When I talk with my child, we are looking at each other's faces and I am at her eye level.

   1 = never   2 = not very often   3=sometimes
   4 = often   5 = always

8. I have my child watch my lips when I make new sounds and encourage him to make them.

   1 = never 2 = not very often   3=sometimes
   4 = often   5 = always

9. If my child does not do as I say, I hold my ground and let her experience the natural consequences of her choice.

   1 = never 2 = not very often   3=sometimes
   4 = often   5 = always

10. When my child says something, I add words to extend what he said.

    1 = never 2 = not very often   3=sometimes
    4 = often   5 = always

11. I expose my child to diverse individuals (e.g., different ages, ethnicities, language groups, religions).

    1 = never 2 = not very often   3=sometimes
    4 = often   5 = always

12. When my child is successful, I praise her effort and hard work, not how smart she is.

    1 = never 2 = not very often   3=sometimes
    4 = often   5 = always

13. I make sure my child socializes with other children on a regular basis.

    1 = never 2 = not very often 3=sometimes
    4 = often 5 = always

14. I teach my child to say "please" and "thank you."

    1 = never 2 = not very often 3 = sometime
    4 = often 5 = always

Total score:

60-70	Outstanding
50-60	Good but could improve
Below 50	Probably need to get support so I can spend more time and effort focusing on my child

In the space below, list the areas you are scoring high in:

In the space below, list the areas where you are scoring low. What can you do to improve in these areas? Don't beat yourself up—think of practical, simple strategies to boost your score for your child's ultimate success and wellbeing! How can you improve? How can you get extra support so you can spend more focused time with your child?